Golf Speak Exposed
The Crazy Things That Golfers Say
(I knew I was gonna do that!)

Chris Gibson

Published by alliebooks.co.uk

alliebooks

Golf Speak Exposed
The Crazy Things That Golfers Say
(I knew that I was gonna do that!)
By Chris Gibson

Published by:
alliebooks.co.uk
A Division of Franology Limited
9 Catherines Close
Catherine de Barnes
West Midlands
B91 2SQ

Parent: 978-1-909429-09-3
ePub version: 978-1-909429-10-9
Mobi version: 978-1-909429-11-6

Second Edition : Revised November 2013   ORIGINAL eBOOKS
orders@alliebooks.co.uk
www.alliebooks.co.uk
ePublished by Original ebooks

a division of Original Writing (UK) Limited - an Original Writing Group company

Cartoon Golfer Images - Shutterstock Library under license ©-Don Purcell
Golf Ball Images - Shutterstock Library under license ©-Schwarzhana

Unattributed quotations are by Chris Gibson
The use of punctuation adopts the British Conventional Approach

British Library Cataloging in Publication Data
A catalogue record for this book is available from the British Library

This book is intended as a light-hearted observation of golf only, not as an instruction book or a definitive scientific manual. The opinions of the author are intended as a monologue and are in no way intended to offend anyone. Any reference to an experience is not directed at any one individual and any reference to an individual by name, implied in the narrative or any association is purely coincidental. The author does not accept any liability in the event that any individual assumes that any reference may be based on that individual.

About the Author

Chris Gibson has authored some serious and some not so serious books since starting to write a few short years ago.

He was introduced to the game of golf at an early age, and had to wait until he was 12 before being allowed to join Robin Hood Golf Club, a private parkland course in the heart of Solihull. As a Junior in 1977 he first learned the game from the late Frank Miller who was a well renowned professional and coincidently the Club Pro.

An average golfer, in truth, this hasn't quashed his enthusiasm for the game of golf or indeed the fun that the social side can provide, while the importance of etiquette and manners on and off the course is just as important.

Putting something back into the game that has given him joy and pain over the last 35 plus years, he has worked in Junior Golf previously and is an active committee member at his own club with the honour of being Club Captain in 2006, at the tender age of 39. Far too young to be a Club Captain, (proud photo below) some said, but apart from contributing to a marriage breakup it was year to remember.
Today there is no issue playing twice at a weekend and it doesn't come with any nag pie anymore.

Away from golf he is a devoted father to a non-golfing daughter (yet) and he embraces laughter in everything that he does, yes even as part of continued committee life!

Follow on Twitter @ChrisGAuthor
Facebook – Chris Gibson Author Page

Contents

Acknowledgments

To Allie, you will be delighted that this book makes absolutely no reference to you at all this time.

To my mother, who still leaves messages on a Saturday or Sunday on the phone asking if I am 'golfing'? Not always mum but it's probably easier to say I am.

To Don, my brother, for the encouragement, one day hopefully you will pick up a club again and we can engage in nostalgic banter on a golf course, just like we did all those years ago.

In memory of Dad, who came out with almost all of the expletives contained in this book as he played a few holes with me as a boy, before sloping off to find a Dunlop 65 or two lost in the rough by another player. His passion was to look for golf balls and to make excuses for his shot making capabilities that were hindered by his, as he would say, "bloody bi-focal glasses!"

To my estranged wife Helen; thanks for the support while I was off doing Captain things all those years ago, I know you never really understood my passion for golf but if you read this you might see why I love the game and everything that goes with it so much.

To the BABS golf society and especially Steve Brown who made the suggestion that I should write a book about golfing phrases as we wandered round Lutterworth Golf Club.

To the golfing partners I have had the pleasure of playing with over the years. Herein might be a comment first uttered from your mouth that I have stored away for this moment, and now share with others.

Chapter One
Why Do Golfers Say Crazy Things?

Millions of golfers all over the World utter lame excuses every day after hitting a poor shot, or they offer apologies for hitting a lucky shot. In return playing partners respond with encouragement or through gritted teeth accept the luck witnessed and pretend that they don't mind. Even if it will cost them the hole or a round of drinks in the bar later!

These verbal outbursts have become clichés over the centuries and now form part of golf dialect, golf culture and the game of golf itself. Of course most golfers are polite and embrace the etiquette that makes it the sport what it is however wouldn't it be great to chirp back after hearing one of these clichés and instead of being polite, simply offer an opinion, just for the heck of it?

This is therefore a collection of over fifty clichés and some satirical replies that golfers would really love to say back. In addition each inclusion has a bit of analysis into what has been said and to highlight just how ridiculous some of the things are that we all say on the golf course in our attempts to justify the reason why we are not on the PGA tour.

On the subject of the televised tour, some of these verbal displays have actually migrated from far away shores to private and pay to play golf courses after being heard on the ogle box. For example we now hear the warning shout "fore" nowadays but with the added "right" or "left" which has itself added confusion to golfers on parkland and links golf courses with nobody at all sure if it is their left or their right that the buffoon that has opened his lungs is referring too. Who in heavens name first decided to add left or right to the shout that for hundreds of years simply warned a golfer of a possible incoming missile? You see it on the course all the time with a golfer glancing to his right after hearing "fore right" and after seeing the hole empty decides it is safe, only to face a near miss as a ball flies in from the left, originating from the hole running parallel to the one being played. Clunk, as the ball hits the electric trolley!

One example of the crazy shouts that come out of a golfers mouth whereby "fore' bellowed is surely enough. Everyone duck, cover your head and nestle behind a tree or that rather large tour bag that has been purchased to improve your scores.

In fact the television has much to answer for in the rapid development of 'golf speak'. Thirty years ago the only real coverage of golf in the UK was courtesy of the BBC, with The Open, highlights of the US Open and a handful of tournaments plus the iconic "A Round With Alliss" that was compulsory viewing in the 70's and 80's for many. Tournament golf had descriptive commentary from Henry Long-hurst, Harry Carpenter and Alex Hay who all provided a very calm description of who was doing what on our screens. The 'godfather' was, and hopefully for many years will be, is Peter Alliss, who added humour and observation to the staid British commentary, for that contribution alone surely it is about time we recognised him as Sir Peter Alliss, for nothing less than what he has done to preserve the balance and decorum of golf compared to the sometimes over enthusiastic commentators that we hear every week on live feeds from the Golf Channel.

With golf available to view almost every day on satellite TV 'golf speak' has evolved far quicker in recent years with quirky comments adopted after hearing them from a guest commentator, "oooh" we say, "a new thing to shout out."

The commentary on the telly must be difficult at times, if not soul destroying, finding something new to say to describe the obvious, "he needs a straight drive here", or "this putt needs to go in"...duh we know thanks. But this doesn't excuse some of these one liners that really don't make sense when broadcast to the masses. Do we question them? No we nod in agreement, are we nuts or what.

"Greens are slowing up - you can see the grass growing"

No you can't, utter balderdash!

Makes no sense at all, but they keep dropping it in at the end of tournaments when the greens slow up. Can you hear yourselves, get a grip!

"He doesn't want to go big here"
I don't suppose he does!

Why on earth would any golfer want to play it over a green, what is it tempting fate so that it does happen and the commentary team can have a giggle or at least something to discuss to fill air time?

"Got out of jail there"
You mean you called it wrong, and he has made par

Didn't see a prison break myself, sorry my mistake the commentator who just said a golfer was dead and buried only to see them make par from nowhere. Phew no deaths and no murderer on the loose!

There are many more phrases that subconsciously golfers have adopted into 'golf speak'. Aside the commentary maybe it is hearing the enthusiastic crowds on the telly, shouting out directions for a ball to "get in the hole". These ridiculous phrases have educated golfers to shout-outs now adopted by the average club golfer. But the culture of hitting a ball and then talking to the ball after it has left the club is a common occurrence and one that every golfer today truly believes will make a difference to the outcome of the ball flight.

But enough of the tongue in cheek criticism of the impact of television on golf courses all over the world, let us move onto the theme of the book and to the funny things golfers say.

One phrase that ranks in the top ten is always the announcement that after hitting a rubbish shot the player will announce "I knew I was gonna do that", so if they knew why didn't they stop and not do it? If we all knew the answer then we would all be as good as each other and the offices and workplaces of the world would have no golfers at all. Instead we would all be playing for millions on the various tours, or even maybe by then just one tour as we would all be brilliant!

The Beautiful Game

This is the beauty of the game, a game that is effectively a man or a woman against the course. With the added problem of self-doubt inside their head.

Most of the problems experienced when trying to hit a little ball around 18 holes boil down small measurements. After all 18 holes that measure 4.25 inches diameter which equates to roughly 14 square inches per hole. A massive collective target of 254 or so square inches which is approximately 1.76 square feet of total area placed into a playing field that is around 4.3 million square feet on average. So if you think about it the target is quite small in truth; no wonder we struggle! The maths aside, the most important measurement is the six inches between the ears.

I, like probably you, don't always use the available six inches 'between my ears' to best effect on a golf course. I have said many of the little comments contained in this book more and more over the years in a vague attempt to probably justify the sheer ineptitude that I have demonstrated on more than one occasion. But like you, perhaps, I still continue to use the clichés even though I hear myself saying them and cringe at what a complete idiot I must sound like to my playing partners.

This banter is what started the whole idea of writing a book, to include what I have said and what

I have heard in over 35 years of trying to get better at golf. I only hope that the rest of the book gives you as much enjoyment as I have taken from the game. The belly laughs that I have had while seeing the reactions from golfing pals after they hit a poor shot followed by an expletive or ridiculous excuse.

The many times when someone has said something and they have collapsed with laughter after hearing what they have just said. Realising that it was a reflex comment that sounded, well, plain stupid. Even times when the serious playing partner has said something and the silence is then deafening as the fear of upsetting him or her by saying anything means that a clasp of a hand over your mouth is more diplomatic.

This is the social side of golf and friends playing together get away with an occasional bit of fun. But a serious match means adopting the etiquette and holding ones gob for fear of offending a stranger or opponent.

While this book is another tongue in cheek look at a subject and the extremes from my over creative mind, it is merely a look at what is said or might be thought when a golfer comes out with a comment to excuse a mistake or fluke shot. It isn't a scathing attack or even an impression of bad sportsmanship on my part. Far from it, more a look at the extremes witnessed from years of playing with different characters and for some of those who have earned the right to fire a comment back without fear of upsetting me, or on the other hand me saying something to a good friend without fear of upsetting them. It is all just banter, but converted into a book of sarcastic and satirical observations.

The fact that I would never dream of saying any of the suggested replies to someone I don't know very well is testament to the same approach adopted by millions of golfers all over the globe.

Most of the time compliments such as, "good shot", "great putt", "well done" and "that's your best today" are said by golfers that now face losing a hole. Witnessing a great shot puts the opponent in a definite winning spot but this courtesy is the foundation for a truly great sport. This courtesy was epitomised by Ángel Cabrera in the 2013 Masters play off against Adam Scott. On the second playoff hole he turned to Scott and acknowledged his second shot into the 10th green with a thumbs up, even though Cabrera was also on the green and slightly further away. With so much at stake, a coveted Augusta National Green Jacket and a Major title, you would expect a nod at best, not such an open appreciation of an opponent also finding the green.

Narrowly missing his own putt and succumbing to Adam Scott who made his twelve-foot downhill count, he was magnanimous in defeat and embodied the essence of what golf and courtesy is. What a great example Cabrera demonstrated to every young golfer, and to a few of us older ones to boot. Therefore although this book is tongue in cheek it is written with a huge respect for the courteous way golf should be played.

That is the wonderful thing about golf, you can play anyone and handicaps even the playing field.

The rules of the game govern the way we effectively self regulate, while manners and tradition ensure a polite approach. Rarely, very rarely do golfers square up to each other and have a full blown argument.

This is what is fairly unique about the game of golf, a gentleman's sport some would say but that would be seen as sexist and this isn't one of my books on 'nagging' so let's just say golf is a game for true sports-people. Golfers are people that at least out-wardly are gracious in defeat as well as success.

Who Are These Golfers?

If you are not a golfer then you probably have no interest in a book like this, and so it stands a chance that you are a golfer reading this. You might be one that picks a club up a couple of times a year or an golf addict that plays every day, it doesn't matter because the game grows on everyone that plays golf. With the challenge of bettering their score or at the very least avoiding heartbreak at the hands of the course or another player that you are matched against.

This doesn't mean that it is a game for 'fuddy duddies' or ex public school types, golf is for all that want to give it a go. Of course in any private club there are standards that are followed by an eclectic group of members that frequent the clubhouse, before and after the main focus on the golf course. Characters that I suppose any club member can categorise and recognise from the descriptions that follow. These are the people that play the game and before anyone says anything they are not based on actual people that I know. Honest, and if you think it is you don't flatter yourself, okay!

First is the novice golfer and then observations on other extreme characters in a club and look at how they can influence our novice in the early days of their membership to an age-old club.

They are possibly the same characters that started the clichés that have now spread to other golfers and so partly to blame for developing a new language, 'golf speak'.

The Novice

Perhaps not new to the game but new to a private club and apart from learning how to navigate a small sphere around a new home course and hopefully improve their handicap, they also have to deal with following the 'rules of the club'. Rules which can be a bit of a culture shock to a them. By definition they might have taken the game up after a few pals did the same and have been nomadic golfers previously; booking tee times at a pay and play or getting up at stupid o'clock to get to the municipal and etch their name down on a starting sheet before returning to the car for a couple of hours kip until the tee time rolls around.

The level of banter and chirpy replies used is wholly acceptable within small regular bands of golfers that move en masse around the country playing a regular fourball. Until one day the collective group or an individual decide to join a club and save on the day rate fees being shelled out every week. After all a golfer can probably get more value by paying a subscription to a club. A club that offers unrestricted play and nullifies the need to get up at stupid o'clock to book a tee time to boot.

In this day and age getting into a private club is far easier than say 30 years ago when waiting lists were evident and stringent checks were part and parcel of golf membership applications. Indeed unless an applicant had at least two reputable sponsors and either a commission in Her Majesties

Forces, a successful business or were from one of the professions many clubs, not Robin Hood mind you, wouldn't even consider an application.

Private clubs have seen supply outgrow demand in recent years and although still 'choosy' many forward thinking private clubs have opened their doors to active golfers, maybe not active club members, but fee payers to balance the books.

But here's the thing, our novice golfer that might be used to more open conversation. Spitting out a gob full of Mars bar when his playing partner carves a tee shot into the Out of Bounds. Now he has to watch his p's and q's if he starts to play with new people that have been around the club since nineteen oatcake. It might be shorted lived until at least our novice develops some banter after working out how serious some members are and whether banter is acceptable or not.

We expect new members to tread carefully and observe the etiquette and for many it is mind blowing that rules about changing shoes in the car park or not donning a pair of jeans in the clubhouse is strictly adhered to. But most accept that these rules and dress code requirements are all part of joining a private club, thankfully.

Reading this, you might think that a 'Colonel Blink' runs every golf club in the land and the draconian standards are out of kilter in today's society; but it isn't the case for the vast majority of golf clubs, it is simply to preserve standards that make the club what it is and avoid ambiguity without prejudice. Wow serious stuff, but this is the essence of being a member of a private golf club. Having and in setting rules it breeds characters not just clones. These characters spice up the experience of being a member and instigate conversation and debate; you have got to love it really.

During the 'probation' period for a novice golf club member the established members definitely discourage outbursts and comments like, "you knob head what was that" immediately after witnessing a scuffed shot or a snap hook. No, instead the long standing member will 'mentor' them, indicating what is 'good form' and what is 'bad form'.

Indeed the novice 'proby' gets lots of advice from fellow members, whether they like it or not. Advice received from these classic type golf club members.

The Know All

The classic 'know all' member is one that has been a member forever and has something to say about everything that occurs, on and off the course.

Maybe they used to be a single figure golfer and now don't hit it as far as they used to but are definitely experts at on course commentary!

They always have excuses for shots that don't quite do what they should have done. They also flagrantly breach the rules of golf, some would say, with friendly advice that instead of taking a three wood that a five iron is the best shot for position. Fine logical advice, but not in a medal round thank you!

Our novice golfer might even scrub their name off a starting sheet if they see the 'know all' has put down to play with them again in the Stableford, thinking "Oh god no not another 18 holes with Butch Harmon's double analysing my every shot, and commentating on his own shots!" God forbid that Brucie tells our novice the bleeding obvious that "Tiger Woods wouldn't have done that."

The Tortoise

No implication of age here because elder statesmen as well as young bucks can get a name for themselves as a slow player that takes an eternity to line up a shot and walk between shots. Pausing every ten paces to take in the view or engage in conversation with playing partners fifty yards ahead.

Whether it is seeing professionals take five hours to get round as the norm on the television nowadays, or that they really think that taking two minutes to set up and hit every shot is actually normal, who knows! Perhaps there is some sort of time warp embedded in their brain that makes them play at a snails pace.

Playing with a 'Tortoise' can be devastating for our novice golfer. Is it normal? They may ask themselves or is there a medical reason that a sub four hour round will bring on a nose bleed? Worse still that a novice is expected to take over four hours to comply with the club mandatory rules.

Now the Tortoise might even suggest that a good piece of advice is to slow down because it isn't good to catch the group up ahead and put pressure on them, but two holes behind is taking slow play to extreme!

Strangely enough the Tortoise doesn't offer too much commentary on bad shots, they prefer to keep quiet and relish the extra shot they have to take. Getting their monies worth no doubt!

The Shark

No not Greg Norman, the golfer who clearly plays off an inflated handicap and protects it in competitions when air shots miraculously enter the game plan so that the score isn't low 60's but just enough to win the silverware or voucher without dramatic effect on the handicap.

The commentary continues on the 18th green after putting out with a monologue on the subject of "it was so close, but for the last three holes", said with the sincerity of a Nazi German Gas Man, moonlighting as a fumigation expert and a shower attendant. For social golf the Shark will happily take money from playing partners and plea 'luck on the day' with the fluky birdies and eagles. Luck? No chance, with lots of holes played quite majestically, three pucker golf shots that amount to a birdie and with the added bonus of a shot to make it 'three net two' was a bonus! The advice from a Shark to our novice golfer here might be to take it easy, fill the trophy cabinet and try and cover the annual subscription with side bets and proceeds from the 'fiddle' winning pot. The fiddle being a common or garden 'chuck up' where everyone is welcome at a set time on almost any day of the week with members turning up to throw a couple of quid in the pot and the winner takes the dosh. Actually 'fiddle' is probably the right word after all for the Shark!

The Militant

Very similar to the 'know all' but a single figure handicapper in the moaning stakes. Someone that regularly challenges the establishment and carries on the commentary in the clubhouse. Bar room moaning using an example of how a rubbish lie cost them a shot or two. Someone needs to be blamed and so let's have a go at the Greens Committee!

If our novice gets in with the militant they can quickly become the gun as the 'militant' loads the bullets for them!

Thankfully the extreme characters are few and most golf club members are 'normal' and love the game, play by the club rules and rules of golf and strive to enjoy their bastion which is found when they pass the electric gate and thus keeping the rest of the world outside.

So, not only does a novice golfer get a plethora of opinions when they join a private golf club, they also have to contend with their own game and develop skills on how to make excuses and say silly things like the rest of the normal membership.

Playing with regular partners or even after playing a few holes with somebody that you haven't played with before gives us an insight into how they usually hit a ball. Most club golfers fade or slice their tee shots and so if they hit it straight or with a draw it is very unusual, but how often do they rattle on about slicing a tee shot as if it was a shot from nowhere? But again tee shots and fairway shots are all included in later Chapters.

Three stabbing every green is soul destroying for any golfer, and the excuses fall on deaf ears if they never do anything about it. What is so true is that if you keep doing the same thing and ignore the angel on your shoulder that keeps saying, "get a lesson" while the little demon on your other shoulder will continue to convince you that it will get better in time, nothing will change. Miracles don't happen in golf that often, but here's the thing, we all yearn for miracles and to hit perfect shots and solid putts every time. Dreaming!

So back to the theme of the book, born out of the fact that these miracles don't happen and that no matter what standard we play the game of golf at there will always be a chance that with frustration or embarrassment we feel the need to explain why the last shot or the whole days performance was not up to professional standard. Let's start with tee shots and what we say and hear on the 1st tee and all the way to the 18th from some players, it's like déjà vu in some cases!

Chapter Two
On the Tee...

Standing over a ball on the 1st tee can be very daunting, especially if a seed of doubt creeps in. All too often memories of hitting a snap hook out of bounds on the left last time or a golfers regular tee shot that nestles in the thirty year old mature conifers on the right are all too likely; just hit it straight we all think, but how often does it go right or left?

The tee shot is after all one that happens every hole. It is repeated on par fours, par fives and those tricky par threes and for most the outcome is far from certain. This poses the opportunity to commentate on the outcome either in an angry outburst, a question to divine powers above, or to playing partners in the hope that an answer is forthcoming and a lesson is learned for the next tee shot.

Do golfers learn from past mistakes? Not likely but we all live in hope!

Oh Pants!

Comments and clichés, like the ones that follow, are in a similar style to other books I have written that have the unspoken answer or reply under the quote. So in this book, I offer an alternative reply to what a partner could say if they were quick enough or brave enough to say it.

Perhaps some might think that it is more 'rude' enough to say it and run the risk of being brought before the Committee for a dressing down!

"Oh no, I've done it again"

Nothing new there then, you would think that by now you know it's your normal shaped shot.

Let's face it if a golfer always hit a fade with the expensive driver that he or she bought last year, then hitting it into the trees on the right is probably going to happen and so saying that they have done it again is really old news that doesn't need to be said at all.

Instead, playing partners come out with a sympathetic reply, make an undecipherable noise or stay silent while maybe thinking what they would like to say. If it happens again on the 2nd and through to the 18th the chances of saying something back increase dramatically but following the rules of golf there really isn't any advice that anyone can give, which moves us onto the second comment heard.

A comment that must rank number one in the all time 'most said comments on a golf course'.

"Why did I do that?"

Because you always do, for god's sake

If you got a free birdie on your card for every time someone asked out loud why they hit the same shot as they always do then you would have the course record. As if anyone can give an answer, never mind whether they know exactly why from looking at a weak grip, a hunchback posture or a flat swing.

Tempting as it is to turn into a closet pro and suggest that they move the ball back in their stance or slow the heck down it is, let's clarify a couple of things. First of all it is polite not to offer advice and second it would be against the rules of golf if playing against someone in match play or stroke play. This however opens up the permitted advice if the poor sod is your partner and so by all means suggesting that they stop playing the ball as if scything wheat is perfectly acceptable.

This being said offering advice to a partner that clearly asks for it when saying "why did I do that?' Doesn't actually mean that they want advice. They may be dealing with gremlins interfering with their swing plane and so to throw another bit of advice in may tip them over the edge. This is quite easy to recognise though if they come out with, "I know" in a short sharp statement. It is probably best to leave them with themselves, with their pain and hope that they recover from the trees to contribute to the hole!

"I knew I should have stopped"

That would have been fun to watch, stopping just before the ball, proper skill that!

What they mean is that on hearing raucous laughter

from the balcony or from outside the pro shop as they addressed the ball, instead of carrying on with their backswing they should have stepped away, glared at the collective group making the din and then set up again with silence prevailing. But they didn't and so stating what they should have done won't help the ball, that is only a few feet closer to the hole now.

On the other hand do you recognise the times when you stand over a shot, line the feet up and complete the address and it doesn't feel right? If it feels wrong then something is pretty much likely to be wrong. But that demon on your shoulder whispers quietly that "nah it's fine just swing at it!" Thus the last thing to go through your mind before scuffing the drive is the first thing that is said after the ball bobbles off the tee peg or careers towards trouble. Why don't we stop? Well, apart from the naughty demon tittering away with drivel and convincing us to carry on we have a concern over the delay in play. By stopping and starting again it can get right up the collective playing partners noses if they like to get round in less than three hours.

I am certainly not advocating the now more commonplace four and a half hour rounds or indeed club golfers circumnavigating the teeing ground for the best stance and then taking three practice swings before standing over the ball for 30 seconds. But if they do and the set up requires a few more seconds than usual or there is a need to stop and start again, then bloody well walk quicker between shots! Yes a faster walking pace might bring on a bead or two of sweat, but think of the benefit of a good cardio workout with brisk walking, let alone getting to the bar quicker.

Ambling around the course is fine if time isn't lost with a two minute pre-shot routine.

That being said taking less than 12.2 seconds to tee the ball up, address, swing and pick up a broken tee peg may be taking it a bit far, and a reason why club golfers mess up if pressured to get a move on. "We need to get a move on boys, they are catching us up", well they will do if they jog between shots, so if followed by the well-known speed golfer trio, 'letting them through' is a good policy.

"Crap! Sliced it again"
Yes you did

Not very much more to say apart from agreeing with the bleeding obvious, apart from some of the insincere comments that paying partners say after hearing the excuse or cliché said in utter disgust that the ball has not gone where it was intended.

Apart from these little gems that are commonplace in a golfers vocabulary there are the specific shouts that roar around the course on medal day. Yells of hope that make absolutely no difference to the outcome unless 'Lady Luck' steps in on occasion.

"No...no...no!"
Err, yes...yes...yes

A golf ball has no feeling of guilt, it will go wherever the face of the club is facing at impact and with the spin that the connection dictates, so why do golfers shout at it as if the little brain inside the core of the ball will take any notice and stop mid flight and correct itself?

Exactly, and so as with most shouted comments it is merely a way of expressing panic in the general direction that a ball is taking. But maybe one-day golf balls might learn to listen! Inventing a legal ball that does would make a few quid none the less.

"Come back... Come Back"
Err, it can't it's gone already

Again, no chance that a ball that has left the teeing ground can miraculously stop and return to the tee, but we live in hope that it will come back, say sorry and then go in the right direction to avoid that penalty shot or scuff the cover as it connects with a bit of tree bark.

"Kick out... Kick OUT... KICK OUT"
Fat chance of it kicking out from that far in!

While a favourable rebound from a tree on the edge of the coppice is probable, kicking out from the centre of the arboretum would mean defying the laws of physics; and so bellowing in the hope that the ball hits a branch with enough force to then miss a bow or ten to pop back onto the fairway is a tall order. Not that a members kick or local knowledge means that it won't of course!

"Miss it... Miss IT ...MISS IT!"
Nope it's right at it!

Whether 'it' is a big Oak tree, a bunker or a water hazard, if a golf ball is heading towards 'it', then it will stand a chance that the ball will disregard the advice and fail to get up high enough or dodge underneath this ending up right in 'it'.

It is 'Sods Law' I am afraid, but the ball shouldn't have been hit towards 'it' in truth, so time to take a slurp of medicine and keep an eye on the surrounding area in the hope that from 220 yards the tears or indeed the onset of glaucoma doesn't cloud the eye and that ball is spotted by a particular tree. This can also save time and the permitted five minutes searching in the 'general area' the naughty ball that clearly has a mind of it's own landed in.

It's amazing how from back on the tee the eye can pick up a white dot amidst the foliage!

"Oh, that's gone"

Yup, saw it too sailing over the white posts, but thanks for clarifying it...Reload?

When a ball flies over an out of bounds line, the sinking feeling is all too much to bear. While some players simply say a few swear words to display ire at the stupidity shown in hitting a ball outside the field of play, others quietly say the obvious as if they are looking down at a monitor and telling millions of viewers what just happened. In fact some people adopt the same tone as a commentator would and after a pregnant pause, they add the word "silly", as if we as onlookers don't realise.

At one down with one to play this can spell the end in a singles match but for a playing partner in a pairs competition the further comment, "over to you" is about as welcome as a sand iron in the groin! "Thanks partner!"

Nearly

These clichés and comments are not reserved for tee shots and can be said after fairway approaches, recovery shots and short iron shots too; as can the following standard replies that we say after a player hits a shot.

So for the rest of the book the comment that a golfer says is followed by an alternative definition or reply a playing partner could say, for a bit of fun!

"Almost"

You still hit a crap shot but thankfully not as bad as the previous one, so maybe it is getting closer to normality.
Yes, a great shot, almost! But whether it was nearly perfect, nearly good or barely acceptable it depends who says 'almost' to the possible meaning.

Is it a bit of gamesmanship from an opponent saying.... 'almost' to throw further doubt into a player's head when they hit their top-drawer tee shot, or 'almost' as they bodge it forwards 100 yards down the fairway, or just reaching the fairway? Or is it a sincere comment, which we would all like to believe that they know it wasn't the best shot but very close to one that deserved a bit of real praise, therefore sportsmanship?

A partner can say it as real encouragement to get a lacklustre performance up a peg or two although maybe the 'almost' is an expression of hope instead as they battle the other two alone?

Who knows but it is still a nice thing to say and ranks alongside regularly used word, "nearly", as a ball shanks off the neck of an iron.

"Good strike"

Caught it well, shame it's off target though
The crisp sound that indicates a clean hit is the most wonderful sound that any golfer can hear, but if the strike unfortunately sends the ball twenty yards off line then hearing "good strike" is little consolation in truth.

Today golfers hope to hit a clean hit more often by using the best clubs available and so shots are aided by a variety of club designs that are a far cry from the heel and toe versus blades that golfers thirty years ago had to choose from. Cavity backed clubs, offset metal's and adjustable heads are common-place, and all claim to be able to lower scores and hit the ball more accurately.

If this is the case why do most club golfers still miss greens and find trouble off the tee? Because no matter how advanced the club and ball designs are today the swing is the critical factor. Swing like an express train, out to in or in to out and connect with the ball a few millimetres outside the sweet spot and the ball strike will sound great but it still goes where it shouldn't. Jeez!

The worst of it is that hearing "good strike" is merely a consolatory comment to the fact that the ball is going to be up a tree stump or out of position, and the opponent that said "good strike" is feeling a tad more comfortable that they will win the hole now.

"Oh, bad luck"

Luck has nothing to do with it, you hit it there and now you will have to pay the price!

Here's the thing, hazards are there for a reason, everyone knows it and so if you hit the ball with the usual power fade and aim left knowing it's going to fade towards a danger area, then aim further left... simple!

Easy enough but if a golfer seems to hit his or her tee shot towards a bunker or overhanging tree every round, then why don't they try something different and hit a three wood short of trouble or aim further left in the hope that the power fade doesn't become a big old slice?

Another simple answer, we want the shot that we visualise to come off, even once every ten attempts and so we keep aiming at the same place and swing the same way to get the same result nine out of ten times only to then appear flabbergasted and risk a coronary due to the shock. What is that all about?

So, when a playing partner says "oh, bad luck" they probably mean 'sorry you hit it in the usual place' or "for god's sake you should know after 30 years that a ball that goes down the right ALWAYS kicks right...sort it out you Muppet."

"Never mind"

Ahh, there you go again towards trouble!

A tee shot that finds trouble is bad enough but the person who hit the ball there is also acutely aware of the problems they will face on the next shot.

Hearing "never mind" is an indication that an opponent or playing partner empathises with the predicament, there for the grace of god and all that, but what they are probably thinking is "poor sod, in trouble again" or "will he ever hit the ball on the fairway?"

No matter how competitive an opponent is, nobody likes to see a golfer hack round the course and miss every fairway off the tee with 'repetitive slice syndrome' RSS, hmmm a new condition for golfers which would sound great on the telly commentary. The only reply to a victim of RSS is, "never mind", meant more often than not, especially at dormie seven.

"You're okay"

It's in play but you're not in the best of places for the next shot!

The relief comment for any golfer that tees off and loses the trajectory of the ball staring to the usual right maybe when they have hooked it, to then have the fellow golfer in the group confirm that the ball is in play, but not the best position is wonderful.

It might be fifty yards short of the normal drive, or that it hit a branch and popped out onto the fairway instead of being buried in the trees and probably up against a root to add to the problem for the next shot.

Whatever the outcome it doesn't matter because it's okay and now closer to the hole without too much of a penalty and thus the next shot will provide them with a chance to make up the lost yardage.

If your opponent states that the ball is 'okay' it could be translated into "lucky sod" instead of course. The polite comment made after an observing one of those lucky breaks and more so if in a match play scenario. The 'luck' means that instead of a certain chip out the next shot could pepper the pin if struck properly. The pressure is back on the now disgruntled opponent when they thought that 'another raider had gone' as the tee shot was heading for trouble, initially.... Bah!

Although the tee shot sets up the hole and defines the next shot either at the green, further up the fairway or from the dark woods, the next shot is just as important and makes the difference between 28 handicap and a single figure player. Or is that chipping and putting? I never get that one right!

Never mind, the next Chapter looks at fairway shots with hybrid clubs, long irons and the difficulty in hitting a straight shot let alone controlling a slice, hook or thin that can sting the hands too.

Chapter Three
From the Short Grass

Not always the short grass, but whether a from the beautifully manicured piece of turf, from the second cut, the scraggy rough or from pine needles under a canopy of branches. When a golfer puts a fairway metal, a hybrid recovery club or a long iron in their hands is a recipe for disaster.

Teeing a ball up on a level piece of turf makes it far easier to hit, no sloping lie to contend with or a divot that the ball is sitting in either. The added problem of the second shot is having a target to go for, be that the green or position. This can really confuse a golfers brain and so when the shot doesn't come off the commentary starts and excuses ooze out of a players mouth. Excuses said just in case the other members of the group would like to know why. They don't of course but thanks for the explanation anyway!

Which Club Then?

So, here we go with another bunch of comments that golfers use and some alternative answers underneath that counter the obvious statement made.

"It only needed a little more"

Then why didn't you take one club more?

We all do it, 150 yards to go and for some bizarre reason we pull out an 8 iron or a 7 wood that from playing week in and week out flies 140 yards. Whoosh, a great looking shot that is right at the pin only to come up 15 yards short and in three-putt country. Then we say, "It only needed a little more" when what we should have done is take a 7 iron or 5 wood instead. When will we ever learn?

"Wrong club, bah"

Hindsight is a wonderful thing isn't it; I could say the same for every shot to be honest.

Probably the most obvious cliché that comes out of a golfers mouth. If it was the right club then it would be pin high or under a foot away, but no, for a variety of reasons that are abundantly clear to any onlooker if the ball isn't stone dead then it stands a chance that the club selection was wrong.

The alternative is that maybe, just maybe, it isn't the club chosen that was the reason for the mistake, it could be the way it was hit, just saying!

Now, choosing the wrong club isn't reserved for the optimum distance required alone. Oh no, the dreaded height factor creeps into the mathematical equation but this is just plain confusing to most club golfers. Picture the tree 75 yards from the green right in line with the shot, to get the 165 yards to the pin then requires say a 7 iron for some but a 3 wood for others, this isn't important because the huge Oak is too high to get over with either and so the best option is to hit a low one perhaps and bounce it in.

What do we do? We hit the 7 iron or 3 wood smack bang in the middle of the tree anyway thinking that we are clever and in so doing adopt the well known fact that trees are 70% air, only to have the ball gathered up and deposited at the trunk.

This stupidity needs explanation and so the obvious excuse is "wrong club". Do we honestly think that the obstacle, or hazard will disappear or is it that our little brains believe that we deserve a break and the club selected will return the faith factor and deliver the shot visualised? Could be.

"Should have played safe"
More hindsight and logic; think I will call you Mr Spock from here in!

For most club golfers the logical thing is rarely done on a repetitive basis and the fact that they acknowledge the safe option after the event is testament to the die hard attitude that gets them into bother 90% of the time. Is it a mini guilt trip that after making a howler and screwing up an impossible shot that they feel remorse for a few seconds and realise that playing safe is a far better approach? Probably but this remorse is short lived because within a few holes the bravado takes over and the logic disappears again and the 'Seve' shot is attempted again.

Some golfers are not Mr Spock at all, they more resemble James T Kirk and follow the gutsy yet risky approach every time, risking all for that extra few yards benefit or the chance to make the putt that saves par. The trouble with this is that the gut wrenching feeling of messing up will result in more than just an over par score, if continually followed our Captain Kirk's will have Klingons to cope with, due to the effect of stress on the bowels!

All of those 0.1's add up to going up in handicap and demotion to the next Division and eventually an inevitable exclusion by handicap from the Club Championship.... Crap!

"Just caught the bunker, damn!"

No you bounced short and into the bunker and let's face it, a divine intervention was the only way that you would have cleared the bunker with a 3 iron from back here!

Bunkers are positioned for a reason and shaped to catch and hold a low flight shot from running through or they have raised humps to grab shots a wee bit short and chuck the ball backwards into the sand. We all know it but 'think' that a little invisible man will catch the ball and throw it where it was meant to go.

The same can be said for the little chip over the bunker with a few yards of green to work with and a landing area of a square yard the ball always comes up three inches short and drops into the sand doesn't it? But more on approach shots in the next Chapter.

This leads on nicely to the next comment and how a ball has the knack of stopping when we want it to roll on and in contrast carrying on when we would really like it to stop.

I am not even going to get into 'spinning back'

because for most average club golfers the only spin we generate is the spin we use to add to our stories.

"Would have been good if it had held on the green!"

But it didn't, did it! It hit the green at 30 degrees and was going like a train, in fact the only thing that would have stopped it would have been a net!

It could be the joy that the target green was hit, for however briefly the ball was in contact with the putting surface, that generates this commentary on how good it would have been if it had stopped. Worse still is when the golfer saying it really believes that the shot had backspin when it clearly had topspin. But that isn't important right now, what is important is that bad luck means that the flat-stick is not needed yet and a lofted shot will be.

"Hit it out the bottom"

I gathered that from the sound and seeing the ball flying three foot off the ground for fifty yards!

Head up equals topped shot and it can happen with any club but hurts when it is a long iron.

The thing is that saying a ball was hit out of the bottom actually refers to the bottom of the club, not out of a persons bottom, thus connecting with the ball, whereby the ball isn't a bottom either.

The poor golf ball, however, being attacked with the lethal edge of the club head will likely actually look like a bottom when inspected on the green. A nice juicy cut that makes it look like an white bottom with a distinct off white crease.

Time to relegate it to the practice ball bag, that makes an appearance once or twice a year.

Surely "thinned it' is more appropriate but stating that it has been hit out of ones derrière is now more commonplace in golf twang.

"I didn't get all of the ball!"
Bit difficult to hit the front as well as the back isn't it?
Where did this phrase come from? It makes no sense at all to state the impossible and the small bit of the sphere that comes into contact with the club face is never going to be all of it...ever!

"I caught it a bit heavy"
What the ball is carrying extra weight?
What it really means is that instead of hitting the ball and a small tuft of grass there is a new open cast mine where the ball once sat on lush grass. For clarification nothing was caught either, how could it be with both hands on the grip, another impossibility!

If we were going to say what really happened perhaps we should say "just gouged the ball forward" or "shizzle, too much divot again!" Whatever the grammatically correct comment after hitting it 'fat' is, the fact remains that the ten inch long divot is evidence enough that it wasn't a clean contact.

"Ahh, winds got it"
Yes it has a tendency when it is blowing hard, which is why the best thing to do is to compensate for a gale blowing left to right!
The funniest thing is seeing a golfer pick a few blades of mown grass up, throw them in the air to see where the wind direction is and then after deciding they hit the ball straight at the pin only to

see it dive right or left on the wind before blaming the wind. You would think that after one round in blustery conditions that the penny would drop, but it doesn't.

The same is true for the shot into the wind and the belief that the normal shot will still get there, before seeing it balloon upwards and do a U-turn before falling woefully short of the target.

There is however the problem of over compensating and aiming too far off the adjusted line so that the alternative plea is "come on wind, where are you?"

Funny how we don't mention the wind when it is blowing right behind and tee shots gain an impressive extra 30% distance or a 7 iron flies 200 yards. Strange that isn't it... must be that the wind had nothing to do with it; it was ability, pure ability.

"Damn, it needs to draw...draw come on!"

Draw, you gotta be kidding me, the last time you drew a ball it was last year when you hooked one drive all season, we called it a draw, but we lied, sorry bout that. Fader's dream of drawing the ball to give them a few more yards distance or a tad more accuracy. A golfer that usually draws the ball might yearn for the fade shot 'option' to help stop a ball on the green.

What is true for the vast majority of club golfers is that they don't have the ability to fade or draw on demand and thus whatever their swing plane dictates will mean they are a fader or a drawer of the little white orb. This being the obvious case, why do fader's tell the ball it needs to draw and those that consistently draw the ball ask for fade? Nuts!

Ahh, but it could be that asking a ball to draw,

for a right-handed player, means "go left" and visa versa for a fade request. Yes that makes sense unless the person issuing the request is indeed a good enough player to draw or fade at will.

Recovery Shots

Apart from the well-known fact that golfers are not actually Superheroes, this doesn't alter the belief that they can pull off miraculous shots and thread a ball through overhanging branches or make the ball impersonate the so-called magic bullet that took out President Kennedy.

Let's face it, a ball pretty much goes in a straight line albeit with a bit of spin to move slightly in the air and so it can't replicate the flight options that Tinkerbelle has at her disposal. Dodging three tree trunks that are equidistant but staggered is a tall order for any Titleist Pro V1.

Any obstacle put in front of a golfer is normally ignored and they attempt to emulate the late great Seve at every opportunity and hit impossible shots and then come out with a bloody good reason why it didn't quite work; excuses like these.

"I was trying to..."
I'm sure you were Houdini

Well that makes sense then, a full description of the intended shot is nice to share with everyone and if it had come off it would have been even more interesting.

But at least they tried, even if the safe shot would have protected the card and taking the medicine and a bogey now appears to be the right choice instead of the triple bogey that is more likely.

"Thought there was a gap!"

Well if there was, you missed it. It's still in the trees but behind you now!

It has never ceased to amaze me that a golf cup shrinks and gets smaller in your eyes the worse you putt, but a gap in the trees suddenly appears to be bigger the more that you look at it. How does that happen? The answer is that it doesn't but with an iron in our hands and a small gap we think that it is simple instead of the reality of the situation which is an ever-decreasing circle due to the faded light in the trees.

Now if you could throw the ball underarm through the perceived gap then that would be fine, apart from a blatant breach of the rules, so why do we think that adding a metre of steel with a forged head on it will improve the chances of threading a naughty ball with a brisk swipe of the club?

It is always the last tree though isn't it; the small gap target is hit with pure skill only to have a pro-truding branch a few feet from the safety of the fairway jump out and bump the ball down or backwards with a mighty thwack!

This annoying error is yet another example of the shortsightedness that golfers have, to see a few yards forward but miss the pending danger a further twenty yards on. Myopia or not, trees clearly have the ability to move in front of a golf ball.

On links courses trees are replaced by other obstacles such as hillocks, gorse bushes and hidden bunkers let alone the god-awful rough that can make a recovery shot back to the fairway a nightmare. From two yards off the fairway a recovery shot is often to get the ball ten yards sideways instead of trying to belt a 7 iron over five yards of rough and onwards to the green. Oh no, every extra yard of rough to clear increases the risk of only 'advancing' the ball into more rough and a physical risk of snapping a wrist in the process. Who needs trees to blame, links rough is just as damaging.

"I should have taken a drop"
Bit late now, but yes that would have been the sensible thing to do!

Faced with the chance, however slim, of punting the ball back into play and still making par with a glorious up and down the alternative is a penalty drop. So, an extra shot on the hole with a couple of club lengths improvement, not nearer the hole of course, not an attractive option for the vast majority of us which is why we opt for the impossible danger shot and the result is more trouble!

Totally understandable if par is nothing less than a must on the last to get into the buffer zone, but not on the 2nd hole. Do we listen to the rational part of the brain? Nope we opt for the ridiculous and end up with a triple bogey, card's Kaput unless an Albatross flies by.

This mentality is the bugbear of club golfers who see a triple bogey as the end of the day after two holes play. No matter how many years a golfer has pounded round a course they know that starting six, seven, six on the first three par four holes means 7:0 to the course and an uphill struggle to finish with a decent score, even off 28 handicap. Thus wasting a shot by taking a penalty drop doesn't equate as the right thing to do. It is silly really because a par streak and occasional birdie can recover the penalty shot…when it happens, which is not often for most of us. So, what do we do? We announce that after now guaranteeing more lost shots that "should have taken a drop" in the hope that our playing partner will say, "oh go on then have another go and take a mulligan." Not going to happen is it!

Of course the alternative to stating a drop would have been a better option is to let our playing partners know that it was so close to coming off, indeed this the next cliché that golfers use as an 'almost' but not quite comment.

"That was almost a career shot"
But it wasn't, no cigar for you then!

Almost is what we humans thrive on, be that we 'nearly won the lottery, nearly married the perfect partner, or nearly found the gold at the end of the rainbow. Golfers are a step up from this and almost do the most wonderful things with a club in their hand. How close a ball gets to nearly going in, a sterling tee shot, nearly scoring a hole in one and almost hitting a recovery shot out of the trees onto the green, just like Phil Mickelson did on the 13th in the Masters in 2010. He did it, so by definition anyone can, right?

Saying that it was 'almost' a career shot is rather silly then isn't it, and more importantly based on what? A clean strike and the ball then resembling a bullet from a rifled barrel, with obviously enough velocity to reach the green...apart from the branch that it caught and deflected it into more branches so that the sound thereafter is akin to a noisy pinball machine.

Because it didn't get to where it was then means that it wasn't a career shot.

While on the phrase 'career shot' what on earth is

it? For amateur golfers it is recreation not a flipping job and so is nothing to do with our careers. But as it is part of golf speak it will remain in our golfing vocabulary.

Let's stick with the one word description, 'almost', which we all hold onto in the hope that it becomes reality one day.

The only other observation on bizarrely calling a particular shot a 'career shot' is to question how many the average golfer gets in his golfing life? Is there one career shot or are there a multitude of career shots available? Hmm, those lucky enough to have this solitary career shot in their teens will have nothing to look forward to unless they are permitted to have many career shots that is, and if so that makes more sense, career shots, plural. Can't wait to have one soon.

Recovery shots aside, the next Chapter looks at the comments made in relationship to approach shots, flicks with a wedge, chips from the side of the green, bunker shots and the increased pressure on any golfer to 'get it close' not leave a nightmare putt.

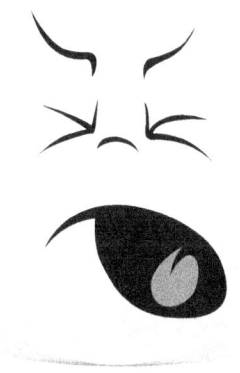

Chapter Four
Be Close!

The business end of any golf hole, to get the ball close to the hole and have a chance of making one putt to save face and record a good score. After the debacle of getting to within a hundred yards of the pin, the chances of making a mess of the approach increase as the golfers handicap is closer to the maximum permitted.

Single figure players often save shots by chipping close and sinking the putt whereby a mid handicap range player might have say a 50:50 success rate. Unless of course there is a disparity in a golfers ability that makes them a demon chipper and putter but a nightmare off the tee and from over 150 yards out! It is the approach is where the shots are lost. Golfers can take three or four, more often than not, and justify the allocated handicap.

Spin In

This is where some classic clichés are spoken by golfers to further explain 'what happened' and give those playing with them even more of the on course commentary to explain 'what should have really happened'.

This therefore the David Feherty bit. Indeed the sarcastic comments akin to those uttered in actual TV commentary which David would pass on to the audience at home and thus out of earshot of the poor player who has skinned a chip through the green. Unspoken replies but still ones that buzz around the minds of playing partners to amuse themselves and divert attention from the same shot they have just played too!

This is just the same as spectators of all types of sport offer opinions on what the participant 'should have done', in their expert opinion of course.

What is it about amateur's that makes them think that they could do any better? It is nuts to hear a bloke in the bar shout out where a football pro should play or throw the ball. Advice that is offered with the benefit of a 50" plasma TV and an abundance of camera angles from a high vantage point and thus with the benefit of full pitch vision brought to the screen from a HD provider.

Okay why not put the 'bar expert' at ground zero with limited vision and watching the game at breakneck speed with a six foot three defender blocking the already limited view. Now make your informed call buddy!

Whatever anyone says it doesn't matter to the amateur pundit? Not one bit because they 'know' what 'he' should have done and 'he' is useless and therefore justifies the expletive bellowed when they get it 'wrong'. So, expert opinion noted it is back to the beer for the other spectators and the hope that the genius keeps quiet. What a font, of knowledge that is, he is!

I suppose it's nearly the same for golfers that spectate from the balcony and observe the slightly less intense if not slower sporting event of golf. Watching the a player finishing up their round and quietly offering opinion to the collective on the balcony that are sipping their own pints.

Whether it is shouted out or whispered the opinion is the important bit, forget the poor sod that is trying to protect the round of the year and make five at worst to card a 67 or to make five to get into the buffer zone. Pressure or what!

Pressure, What Pressure?

The pressure of the approach shot can ruin any golfers card; pressure that is not down to anyone else in truth, more pressure born out of the self-doubt placed on the golfer by that little demon on the shoulder again, "don't mess it up, ahh you probably will!"

No matter what standard of golf you play there will be pressure at some stage in a golfers life and on more than one occasion. Just think on the huge pressure that a pro must be under to keep it going and make the cut. Nothing compared to the pressure on the last day of a tournament to card a par round to win a major after doing the hard work on the previous three days to lead by six.

I can't imaging how that must feel, but in my own little world the pressure of recording a safe score for the last three holes has flummoxed my mind so many times that I care not recall them all.

But here is one recollection to share, not that I am scarred by it! Not much!

T'was a sunny day, perfect conditions and for 15 holes utter joy, level par gross off 15 handicap; a wonder round opportunity, until I finished 6, 6, 9 and dropped ten shots to finish with a net 67 and lose a Wednesday Open by one shot.

Pressure? No, more like meltdown and boy the clichés that came out that day, all to no avail. Alas a similar repeat performance a year or two later but with an improvement thankfully to finish 5, 5, 8! Losing by a couple of shots this time. What an arse!

Where were the shots lost in that first meltdown? You got it, the approach shots, two to get out from the green-side bunker on the par three 16th, two again from the green-side bunker on the par four 17th and both followed by three stabs on each green. The 18th was all down to the approach after a blinding tee shot, a 4 iron hooked into the trees, "no, no, no…come back, come back, come back!"

But alas it was too late, the result was a lost ball, "should have played safe" came out of my mouth, and so a penalty drop and distance and the 'safe shot', with an 8 iron short of the green. I had still only played four and in my mind to get up and down would be nice to finish six and only drop another two shots and card a 64. But alas no, the approach from less than a hundred yards came next, a 'chunked' wedge, "didn't get all of the ball", was the next cliché said to my now embarrassed playing partner. The result was a pitch that came up short, "what am I doing?" came next and silence from the poor sod that was trying to keep score too. What finally followed was a third consecutive three stab. After the obligatory handshake with a playing partner, who managed a, "hard luck, but well done," not sure whether to console or congratulate me, bless him. There was empathy and obligatory silence, after the courteous 'thanks for the game'. One word from previous Chapters works here... 'Almost'

A story for the 19th hole and a range of excuses that now years later have been committed to text to secure the story to the annals of golfing legend, albeit for an average golfer that nearly had a net 60 if I had only bogeyed the last three holes instead. Yep 'almost' but at least it avoided being cut to 10 in one fell swoop, the only solace in a traumatic story!

After reading this I bet you have one of your own that has scarred your memory, the round that will either have a story of a bad finish or an incredible recovery after dropping shots in the first few holes, I guarantee it.

Almost!
But enough of self-flagellation for the author, let us continue to the cliché's and comments said by golfers that resonate around courses and from a hundred yards or so in from the green. Replies in Fehertyesque style that regular partners might say and strangers might think but not say out loud.

"It only needed another ounce"
Another ounce of what? A bigger ball that weighs more, sorry don't get how weight makes any difference to the shot, more weight equals more force to move it, so perhaps it's down to force, which isn't weight by the way, just saying!
The real translation or definition is that the shot

needed a little bit more and while a smart arse could explain with physics that the desired result is actually down to Newton's First Law.

What I hear you say?, well if you want to get all technical, imparting force on an object 'at rest' which in this case is the ball, and moving it with a lump of metal that weighs more than the object, the club that is, the result is to then set the object in motion. Newton's First Law, see!

So, being a man I am trying to explain it and fix the whole damn phrase. Okay maybe the comment unbalanced requirement is reference to the extra ounce is the weight of the club, in this case the mass of the club head. If I have got this right then the quick answer is to bung some lead tape on next time to get the extra ounce, but be careful it will likely need a few rolls of self adhesive lead tape to make any difference and turn an 8 iron lofted club into a deformed heel and toe replica. Or maybe just take a 7 iron next time eh!

"Be good"
Oh god I hope it is too!

From nowhere a good shot can leave the club with potential to pepper the pin. From the moment the golfers head slowly lifts the vision is beautiful.

The slow motion vision of the ball doing what it is meant to and fly straight and true is a moment when a flutter enters the tummy region and a feeling of invincibility reigns for a few seconds.

Instead of shouting 'yay, at last', a level of decorum prevails and, just like the pro's do, a cool and calm "be good" is said instead. Part of this display of controlled emotion is to make sure that playing partners are paying attention and watch in slow motion too and thus see the epic shot. More likely so that they can applaud and possibly even congratulate the 'duffer come good".

While "be good' is an innocuous and completely inoffensive comment, when you break it down what is good anyway? Is it good if it makes the green, good if it lands and holds to within a foot of the pin or good if it ends up in the hole? Whatever good means to a golfer the wonderful thing is that for a brief moment in their golfing career they can take in the moment and for the time the ball is in flight, until it finishes, there might be an outstanding outcome to make up for the less than fantastic majority of shots. It's what brings us back time after time.

"Be lucky"

Oh god it's 50:50, he could do with a break, come on stay up... Oops get down!

When a golfer shouts, "be lucky", it usually means that a freak of fortune might have to intervene to compensate for the errant direction and that well-known hump is needed to kick the ball back towards the pin location.

On the other hand it might refer to the need to stay up and clear the top of the bunker or hold on a tier of the green and not dribble back to the front or side of the green for that nasty putt. Either way "please god, for once today, be lucky!"

Positive Thinking

For a moment let us stay in the positive clichés and relive the times when shots do come off and visions of becoming a scratch golfer almost appear as real as the recurring dream that plagues sleep.

Luck is an unproven characteristic of golf, after all how can it be measured, what is the sample size and who defines the criteria? The myth of good luck for some and bad luck for others is actually down to hitting the ball in the general direction required. Luck, if it were real, would also have to navigate all of the external constraints that get in the way of a golf ball; the randomness of a swaying branch. Where a sprinkler head has been installed, the gust of wind, when the grass was cut or even the angle of approach.

Yes we all have favourable bounces and we even hole out from an approach shot once in a blue moon, thanks to the flag stopping a ball instead of the white missile rolling twelve feet past.

Is it luck? If you want to believe that it is then fine, but surely it is the 'rub of the green' and a good result from the Chaos Theory that defines the small tweaks that can affect a ball, even down to a blade of grass or lump of sand on the green.

What is abundantly clear to all golfers is that whatever people class as luck, again good or bad, there are some players that seem to get more than their fair share, and probably part of someone else's share to boot. We all dismiss the scientific evidence and put it all down to one word, because it fits... luck.

"Sorry about that"

No your not, and why should you, rub of the green old bean.

After all of the excuses that are used to explain why things haven't gone right for the attempted shots in a round, where on earth does an apology fit into genuine golf speak? Sorry for a shot that bounces short of a bunker, hops to the top of the mound and rolls down to six inches? Sorry my arse, people are not genuinely sorry when they say it and why the hell should they? Accept the outcome as 'rub of the green' and however gracefully an apology is said or taken it will not change the outcome, if offered take the conceded putt and bask in the moment; for once you deserve a bit of luck; oops there I go again.

Golf has a way of balancing out good fortune, we all know it and for every skulled chip that hits the bottom of the pin and drops in, there will be a perfectly executed chip that stops an inch short or horseshoes the hole. From Chaos Theory to Ying and Yang, and yes even the lucky buggers who seem to get more than average will have their comeuppance with a missed putt from under two feet or a double hit from a delicate chip.

This doesn't stop some feeling hard done by though and we blart out a partly disguised demonstration of utter disgust, born out of jealousy.

"You jammy bugger"

Thanks for that, yes it was wasn't it; shall we count up your jammy shots while we are on the subject? No? Didn't think so!

What it really means is, "I can't believe it, from nowhere, how did you manage that?" As long as it is said in a friendly manner then fine and all part of banter, but if someone says it with a venomous undertone they ought to be careful as with venom there is often found a forked tongue.

Expressing disgust is deemed as 'bad form' in the game of golf and a regular moaner is often chastised by his or her playing partners and faces playing golf as a one ball, if not careful. This doesn't stop the 'ranter's' in fact maybe I should have described the type in Chapter One, but we all know what they are anyway, at a golf club or not. They are the people that tell you what they think or will do and then forget what they have said five minutes later or don't do anything! You know the one's that you say "yeh, whatever" to out loud or in your head. "Ahh he's off again...." Joy!

The Sweet Spot

The all too rare bit of good fortune is replaced with misfortune all too often for most of us. We might even keep score of the perceived good luck and bad luck we experience on the course. A mental score that clearly proves that we are 'unlucky' compared to other golfers whom always get a good kick and hole fluky putts.

With approach shot's the margin of error might be the same as for a tee shot or full long iron, however it appears that the margin of error decreases the closer we get to the green. For some reason the margin of error appears to reduce as the loft of the club increases!

Is it true, probably not but it is one heck of an excuse! For now let's pretend that a driver or three wood might allow for a few millimetres, if not a centimetre or so of variance in finding the sweet spot to improve and increase the quota of decent drives. Unfortunately a wedge shot feels like the sweet spot has a variance of less than two millimetres on the club-face and you have had it if you are outside the perfect contact point!

Club designers will be up in arms at this assumption, Karsten Solheim will be turning in his grave, and they, and he, would be right to be so outraged at this claim. What I am saying is that clubs compensate quite a lot, but it 'feels' like it has to be perfect in the hands of an amateur golfer. The reason we 'feel' that it has to be perfect is that the ball doesn't always go in the right direction, desired trajectory or the required distance, therefore the club is too sensitive, obviously!

Further evidence, in our distorted minds, is that the 'almost' perfect shot which is occasionally only slightly out of the sweet spot area often ends up with a cataclysmic result. It is the golfing phrase that ranks alongside having to say 'the Scottish Play' in thespian circles. Can we quote it? It will probably cause bad luck in our next round, but sod it here we go, 'the shank'. How can the game be so cruel to have such a gut wrenching shot that has a distinct possibility of happening every time we pull a short iron from the bag?

Commentary is limited from the golfer who has one of those shots, I'm not writing it twice as that would be fatal to my already precarious game at the moment. So let's just say the one that rhymes with 'tank' (parental guidance is required in this word association game, especially with junior golfers part of the target audience for this book, thank you).

There isn't a cliché or any excuse that would be worth saying and so the best way to describe the aftermath of a 'tank' is a rush of blood to the face and a look of shock coupled with another word that rhymes with 'hit' or another that rhymes with 'truck'.

Indeed on the subject of 'tanks' that is all I care to say, apart for a plea to feel sorry for the golfer who has more than two on a day, as with all 'tanks', two is wrong and there is always a chance that a golfer may get labelled with being a 'tanker' if they have more than two 'tanks' a day.

By the way the myth that everyone is given a set quota, a bit like a bucket full, thus the quicker and more often you have a 'tank' the quota will be used up and your bucket will be empty has never been scientifically proven.

So in conclusion, I urge all golfers to avoid 'tanking' on the course as it will not only offend but make you look silly and likely cause acute embarrassment, especially if playing in a mixed match. Thank you, that is all on the dirty subject.

The 'chunked chip' is probably the worst bad shot a golfer makes. Hitting a divot only to see it go further than the ball is not a good sight. Even if the ball beats the divot in the length race it usually comes up far too short of the desired landing area and then in an attempt not to hit another chunk a golfer has more chance of skinning the next one through the green, or taking an innocent playing partner's shin bone out.

The short game is indeed the soul-destroying part of any golfers game. A confident and competent golfer that can chip and putt will make those with less confidence and ability feel the need to make an excuse here and there after messing up an approach, and likely spur the following clichés.

"Just my luck"

Or is it that the bad luck you keep wittering on about?
Luck has naff all to do with it, as I have suggested already; a 70% shot has a 30% chance of being off

target, be that short, long or with the required spin to stop close to the cup. We all say it is down to luck, yes playing partners too saying "bad luck". In the real world people would say why it failed to happen, however on a golf course we politely say the right thing, while thinking something completely differently. Oh, how lovely it would be to have a pairs partner take the pressure off by getting on the green only to witness 'bad luck' and a missed green and then pile the pressure on to do much better. Maybe the next shot will have better luck eh!

"No sand in these bunkers"

Yes there is I can see it, golden and grainy, have another look.

The fact that the shot has left the club-face at 60 mph and is now heading for the lovely patio windows of the house that backs onto the 6th green is irrelevant. It wasn't the golfers fault it was down to the lack of sand in the bunker, in their mind. But then to come out with a lie by saying there was 'NO SAND' when there clearly is 'SOME SAND' is not only descriptively incorrect but it doesn't mean a free hit.

It is frustrating none the less to first test the sand out by treading and wiggling the golf shoes to see how deep the sand is only to play the shot off a few millimetres of sand cleverly disguising rock hard compacted sand beneath. Instead of flopping the ball up with backspin the club-face bounces and causes the leading edge to do it's worst. From a gracefully planned escape the resulting shot is more reminiscent of a hockey shot from the edge of the 'D' out towards the other sides goal.

It is a bad shot to see especially a ball traveling at Mach II at quail height over the putting surface. Another reason for golf insurance by the way.

Caution is needed when describing the course of events on a claim form as the assessor would likely contest the description that there was 'no sand' in the bunker and take issue after the event. No point in trying to blame something that could be proven false in less than a few seconds.

Where There's Blame, There's A Claim

On the subject of insurance claims and the things that golfers use as excuses to appeal liability, I bet there are some humdingers that the insurance companies have received over the years. Not that I am privy to any but with the golfing twang that we all use nowadays, surely there must be some excuses that have caused a titter or two when blame is clear straight away. Today there is a selection of golf insurance policies available to cover theft, hole in one bar bills, damage to property and for inadvertently taking an eye out.

Years ago golf insurance was part of the house contents policy and claims were dealt with by assessor's that were used to burst pipes and the loss of the VHS video player, and so would likely be baffled by some of the golfing claims submitted.

Descriptions written in golf speak using words like thinned, sliced and detailed affidavits such as "I am a habitual hooker, my shiny balls often end up in the school playground, I never mean any harm and indeed the kids would help me", can you imagine reading this without any 'golf speak' knowledge? Totally understandable to do the right thing and call the crime unit.

Thankfully today specialist underwriters for golf insurance policies recognise this terminology and avoid summoning the authorities.

There are probably many real reasons that refer to golfing excuses for a wayward shot that has left a dent on a bonnet, obliterated another roof tile on the house on the corner of the course that gets frequent ball abuse, or to why a club member now requires daily care for a month or two after been mown down with a Srixon from 30 paces.

Lies and Lies

Aside from the lack of sand in a bunker there are some other standard excuses, clever excuses that make absolute sense to state a valid reason for the cock up. At least valid reasons, in a golfers own opinion, reasons conditioned into a golfers mind after years of spewing excuses and blame for having a shocking game.

"Had a crap lie"

Did you, oh bless.

Here's the thing on such a vast playing area there will always be a chance that the ball will come to rest in a nasty place. Places like the acorn infested and light starved ground in the dark wood that a ball is attracted to.

Just like iron filings are attracted to a magnet, an errant tee shot is seemingly attracted to the only bit of sparse turf next to a bunker with lush grass all around. Coming to rest on a crappy lie may make the golfer wish that the ball was in the bunker instead, whether the bunker has sand or not.

Even landing on the fairway is no guarantee of a

perfect lie. An unrepaired divot hole or aside a twig, that cannot be removed for fear of moving the ball, can pose a problem and a ready made excuse, and quite rightly too, what bad luck!

The beauty is that a golfer who likes to make an excuse here and there can always use the crap lie alibi due to the fact that most of the time his or her playing partners are a fairway away and can't see if it is a bad lie or not. Brilliant really.

The other good thing is that if a ball is first lost and eventually found after four minutes or so the chances that it will be buried and in a bad spot mean that the playing partner that finds it will pre-sell the bad lie excuse by saying, "here it is, but you are not going to like it".

In both cases, bad lie or not so bad or whether it has been seen by a playing partner or not mean that a golfer can blart out the excuse after the ball has been hit badly. A golfer can tut, look at where the ball has just been and state the perfect excuse "crap lie". It's pure genius to use a bad lie as an excuse by saying a little lie too.

"Did you see that?"

Couldn't miss it, it nearly took my left ear lobe off!
A mindful golfer will realise the danger that a golf course can pose and it makes sense to especially keep an eye on those closest to you.

This cautious approach is also part of the game, to watch a playing partners shot so that they can keep their head down over the shot so when they ask if "you saw that" it stands a very good chance that you did, a bit of a wasted comment really It is just asking for sympathy, again!

It doesn't help if you have commented on the shot

as a "nice one" only to have to add "aww, shame" at the end as it takes a kick or scoots off the putting surface.

Empathy and opinion rarely mix in golf, it is either one or the other that is adopted. Courtesy means that in most cases it is empathy that is portrayed all the way to the green and despite the banter that includes opinion.

The dodgy ground is the green where up to four players congregate and pass comment and say clichés well within ear shot and with nowhere to hide. Which brings us to the next Chapter, putting.

Chapter Five
Get In The Hole!

The green is where the culmination of a golfers efforts and the trials and tribulations of the previous few hundred yards progression offer the chance to make the effort count and record a decent score for the hole. Not always a decent score if the crap lie, 'tank' or penalty drop have cost unwelcome shots. However the green offers the chance to sink a putt and save face as 'hope' for every golfer. It also presents the opportunity to add more shots to the score and end up with the feeling of betrayal at the hands of the course.

The frustration a golfer experiences on the green is normally just after the putter face dispatches the ball in the general direction of the hole. A pretty good indication of frustration is the vehement comments said by the most placid of golfers. This also provides more opportunity for onlookers to offer a witty retort or at the very least smirk at a thought that might give some internal pleasure, a 'real day-brightener' on a poor day on the course for them as well. Naughty I know but sometimes the excuses offered and comments made are the pinnacle of golfing clichés that make no sense at all.

Poor putting can be just as damaging as chunking a chip. There are some very good reasons why a putt goes astray, such as from the peppering of a green every day and the pitch marks, that people don't repair properly. The inevitable spike marks caused by golfers that shuffle along dragging their feet instead of stepping like normal people is another obstacle and even sand on the green from the bunker that doesn't have any left in it! Yes, these real reasons to deflect a well struck putt have some merit and perhaps even rival other excuses from the bullcrap department. Whatever excuse anyone uses on the green the reality is that hitting a bad putt means that it won't go in the hole.

Rolling, Rolling, Rolling

Let us first look at the things that are said to finally try and make the ball do something that it simply cannot do, while rolling towards the hole.

"Go, go, GO!"

Certainly needs to, it's halfway and dying as I speak.
Decelerating on a putting stroke is the normal symptom. Common especially when a golfer is not sure of the speed of the greens and whooshes the backswing a foot behind the ball. Panic then sets in and in a millisecond the brain calculates that if the follow through is struck with the same tempo,

the ball is going to launch off the green and maybe even into the bunker again! Decelerating is the result and leads to a weak putt that dribbles off line or way short.

We are advised by golf gurus to always get the ball to or past the hole, with the reason being that 'never up is never in', a cliché that makes sense for once.

It can be painful to watch and then cast some doubt too if you are up next and on a similar line as the putt just witnessed comes up ten feet short. Ignoring the stubbed putt is best policy and to use a bit of 'noggin' to ensure that you are not conned into thinking the green is slow and fire a your effort eight feet past.

Thankfully recognising another golfers 'sheer ineptitude' on the green allows a player to ignore the putt hit like a cover drive; sorry digressed to cricket, as a guide of the pace of the green. Ahh yes nothing worse than playing with a golfer that demonstrates 'sheer ineptitude' in all departments, apart from being accused of the same for one bad shot in an otherwise faultless round. Thanks by the way Fred for the 'ineptitude' comment a decade ago! It will stay with me for a lifetime and provide John and Willo with a recurring laugh on the classic one liner until we all kick up daisies.

"Whoa, Whoa, WHOA"
Jeez, incoming!

The usual phrases, such as "taxi for Gibson", or "shall I chuck the flag down behind the ball?" are however 'acceptable' comments from the regular playing partner attending the flag. Especially if the speedy effort narrowly misses the flagstick that was hurriedly wrenched from the hole with a bit of a panic.

Have you ever had a flagstick jam in the hole when attending? Yes and also risked the potential for a golf injury by twisting the spine or pulling a muscle trying to get the flag out of the hole? It's a dangerous game.

Over exuberance or an attempt to save par are reasons for whacking a putt too hard of course, but reading the green and working out the effect that the slope or grain becomes a pure maths issue, and we all know how maths can confuse us, don't we!

This mathematical appraisal doesn't take into account a golfers inability to recognise an uphill or downhill putt in many cases. Crouching down behind a putt and concentrating on the left to right slope while using a putter as a plumb-bob sets the brain off on the Calculus bit only to forget to work out whether the incline is as dramatic as it might be. The result is a great putt on line but woefully short, oh bummer!

After a few misread putts the classic cliché is said as a generalisation of the greens.

"I can't get these greens today"
Ahh, Confucius reigns and the net result is that you haven't got a clue, have you!

Lining a putt up is a science and one that just like the mathematical problems we had at school with algebra where 'some just get it and others just don't get it at all', working out the line and what the slope will do is akin to almost getting the right algebraic formula but with a little mistake in the final calculation. Science, pah, it will baffle us to the end.

If the first green throws up a problem and a misread speed or 'turn' then it stands a chance that by the 4th green a golfer will have no idea of how to read speed or grain. This is worse playing on other courses instead of the regular home club and especially if a golfer is used to say 10-11 on the Stimpmetre at home and they play on another course with a mix of 8's and 13's. It is bound to bamboozle the brain.

Fast greens become places to fear and timid putts roll and deviate off the ideal line and gain pace after the hole Sphincters work overtime and a three putt is a godsend. Slow greens ruin a smooth putting stroke and a 'hit and hope' mentality often provides a titter or two from playing partners, let alone the divot taken out of the green occasionally!

Worse still is if the playing partners are competent putter's and clearly the ones that got algebra at school. There flawless putts glide over the surface and dive into the cup from all over the greens, short ones long ones and lags make your efforts seem, well pathetic in truth. To remain focussed they will often ignore the excuses made about your putts and zone out after a few holes, reluctant to attend the pin probably as there is no chance that you will be anyway near.

By the 17th and after taking 39 putts already, the joy of holing a thirty footer from just on the green can mean collective elation for everyone and is something to behold. With now 40 putts in total a golfer may even come out with a final comment such as, "there, finally got the pace!" Okay a bit late in the day but for a playing partner that has witnessed a meltdown on the greens for the last three hours all that can be said in reply is "bout time, thank the lord!"

Yip, Yip

Putting has a tendency to ruin the enjoyment of the game and spread like an infection through the rest of a player's game. Putting is a roller-coaster experience for most golfers throughout their life, indeed good putters get worse and bad putters improve, albeit briefly for some.

We see it on the televised pro events too with professionals that develop problems on the greens and move down the rankings missing their opportunity to win a Major, all because of putting.

If it can hamper Sergio Garcia or Lee Westwood, then it can certainly hamper an amateur's game too. For those have a putting affliction the 'yips' mean an extra five or six shots per round on average which can turn a 69 into a 74, ahh yes that is why a golfer is off 13 and not 7 or 8.

For anyone reading this that doesn't know what the yips are, in very basic terms it is missing three-foot putts regularly, whether pulling the ball or pushing it past the hole. How bleeding annoying is it to do the hard work with a green in regulation to take three more to get it in the hole? Very.

Using the word 'yips' to make an excuse is nearly as bad as using the 'tank' word and thus golfers shy away from discussing or saying 'yips' for fear that they might become infected too.

It's that luck thingy again, a 'yipper' is obviously an unlucky putter.

In an attempt to eradicate the 'yips' a golfer will try anything be that a new grip, left hand below right, the index finger down the shaft, the index finger on the front of the grip i.e. the claw grip or any manner of combinations. No matter what grip style is adopted, changed and changed again the fundamental reason is identified as the equipment used.

It is not uncommon for a golfer to have an old bag in the garage or potting shed with a variety of putters. An enviable collection of original Ping Anser's, an Odyssey Two Ball, Zebra and even an old John Letters used as a Junior. With all of the collection of putters relegated to rust over time until called upon for a brief appearance for a week or two until another new putter is purchased from the club professional.

The 'Aladdin's Cave' of new shiny putters is more often well positioned in the pro shop to entice a struggling golfer to pick up and try out the array of blade, belly or mallet style. Even the latest 'ding dang do' technological effort with ugly yet essential protruding metal bits to balance the monstrosity and generate roll and a perfect strike. All well and good but it might be advisable to turn it upside down in a golf bag and avoid the risk of impaling oneself unless a padded putter cover is supplied.

Golf magazines cleverly review and rate new putters that also promise improvement, just the same as the latest irons and drivers, but again, sorry Mr Solheim, it is the confidence to hit the damn putt that is essential. Instead of buying a new putter the money could be better spent on, say a dozen copies of this book to give out at your club to give golfers some new clichés to use on the greens. Not a bad idea that, spread the word will you, thanks.

In a nutshell the only answer isn't a new Anser, but practice and persistence with a putter that feels right. How often do amateur golfers spend and hour or two bent over their balls, on the putting green to develop a nice stroke? Once in a blue moon is the overwhelming response I bet. Or they only spend a few minutes practicing before walking to the 1ˢᵗ tee in most cases. Is it any wonder that the putting then generates the vast majority of excuses and clichés on a golf course? Exactly, which reminds me I need to recover the old putter from the 'everything golf bag' that has a few drivers and a selection of putters and practice my putting because it is dreadful.

Caps Off

After holing out on the 18ᵗʰ the mandatory hand-shake is the last chance on the course for a player to utter a final excuse or cliché.

Thanking an opponent for the game is the proper and courteous thing to do and should be the last thing that is said. However some golfers can't resist the final apology for the performance and I suppose this is one of the nice things about golf. It could be an apology to a partner for letting them down or to a fellow competitor that marked the card for holding them up and for submitting them to a barrage of excuses and commentary.

Once the game has finished playing partners will occasionally offer empathy to the struggling golfer for a bad day on the course and even encouragement that next time their luck may change and the score or result might be slightly better.

This leads on nicely to the final Chapter and the things that golfers say in the clubhouse and much like the golf pundit's do during those rather annoying commercial breaks that the US golf channels have every five or six minutes, an analysis of what could have been. Off we go to the 19th hole.

Chapter Six
What Are You Drinking?

S hoes off, clubs thrown into the locker or the car boot, a quick change of clothes and using the nailbrush to remover the residue of the course from the fingernails, it is off to the patio, balcony or the bar to buy a round and talk the talk.

Changing and having a bit of solitary time is a chance to review the round in your head. A bit like watching a repeat of 'Lost', you might have seen it once before but fast forwarding through the episode is always an option at X6 on the Skybox, stopping at the interesting bits to review at normal speed.

Hole by hole the extra shots are counted up and the 'hindsight approach' to what shots could have been saved and the effect on the final net score or what it would have done to the match score.

Reviewing a performance for improvement is fine, identifying where a lesson could help eradicate the chunk chips or 'yips'; however lots of golfers don't review for any potential improvement, they only review for a tad of mental adjustment and thus convince themselves that the submitted score for the medal or the match just lost 3&1 is a dream...or the result should have been different, with a bit of luck!

The key moments of the last four hours on the course are identified and between dumping the clubs and electric trolley in the boot, the subject matter for the 19th hole is planned. God's help the playing partners, if the disgruntled golfer prepares a 'Golfing Gettysburg Address' to round off the day.

Synopsis Time

Off the course the rule on giving advice is nullified and here playing partners can offer opinion, as a closet teaching pro maybe. It can be quite amusing to overhear or participate in post round discussions with golfers coming out with some more clubhouse clichés, but this time getting both barrels back, if they deserve it.

"You were lucky on the 12th kicking back into play"

Lucky my 'Harris' it brushed the branch and carried on you cheeky git.

In some golfers 'opinion' a ball that kisses a few leaves is defined as kicking out from the bow of an Oak tree. Yes they actually believe that a '45 degree' deviation occurred instead of the yard shift in the flight of the ball. It was clearly luck, the same luck that evaded them all day. How rude.

Any golfer that suggests that an opponent had a huge kick off a tree, when it was just a small clip of a leaf, is looking to incite debate and probably then use the debate to bring the conversation back to the misfortune of their game. Just saying!

With an average golfer playing upwards of 80 shots in a round, why do some concentrate on when an opponent had one or two lucky shots, and not on the 78+ normal shots, likely mixed in with a few duffer shots? Because it justifies the moaning and claim of having no luck compared to the opponent. It is madness, but will never change!

"The turning point was that long putt on the 16th that hit the hole and dropped in"

We were 2 up at that stage and the firm putt dropped in, but I concede it hit the hole…at the bottom of the cup! Forget that the 'ten footer', described in the comment, was for a half in three and that the golfer making the statement had pulled his tee shot into the lake and thus bugged out from any participation. Indeed it was fair pickings and justice as 'his' partner had chipped in for three after chunking a chip first.

No, the turning point was going two up on the 15th with a birdie, certainly not a fluky half on the 16th. What planet are you on?

This further reinforces the fact that golfers that look for pivotal moments in a match or a medal round as 'the reason' are clearly narrow-minded and don't actually see what is abundantly clear to everyone else. Quite sad but actually brilliant if you think about it because otherwise they would probably over analyse their game and decide to put the clubs in the potting shed to rust with the collection of putters that live in there already.

"I really need to sort my putting out"
Ya think?

A regular partner may have been witness to this common comment at the 19th hole for many years now, and deep down they hope that one day, just one the comment is missing from the post round discussion. Get a lesson with the pro, for all of our sakes.

For the golfer who clearly has a putting problem but does nothing about it, they actually believe that this is the first round that it 'all went wrong'. A bit of a surprise today that putts didn't drop, wake up and smell the coffee!

"What you need to do is…."
Oh, crap the 'know all' has a clubhouse lesson for me!

What is funny is that the 'know all' actually played with another three partners, all, of which have made a speedy exit after a round to avoid his ranting. The 'know all' was in the following group and from half a hole back he can miraculously analyse your swing and offer opinion. How does that work?

The four gathered around a table, sipping 'rock shandies' to quench the thirst, are joined by the 'know all' with a third pint of lager on the go and no one to talk to, so he pulls up a chair and makes it five. Without invitation he offers advice, "I saw you on the 13th, you played the wrong shot for your second, should have been a 5 iron", and this is déjà vu from the social game a few months ago. He might then offer additional expertise, "you're still swinging a bit flat, told you about that already", why thank you, you may think!

The conversation inevitably turns quickly into what the 'know all' has done today and becomes a monologue with every hole described, the good or bad, but still a hole-by-hole description of every shot. A box of matches is a useful aid here to pin open the eyelids, but if there are none available a couple of broken wooden tees from the pocket work as well. By the time he describes the last putt on the 18th and if you haven't slit your wrists by now, the important concluding synopsis is that "but for a bit of luck the course record would have gone today" What, again that has to be the third time he has said it this month!

"I know where I was going wrong"
This should be good, go on then

In an attempt to get the conversation back to the actual escapades for the relevant fourball, and thus take the conversation back from the 'know all', one player might offer up his thoughts on the round. It could be a slight swing adjustment that would help, positioning of the ball in the stance or slowing it down as the analysed improvement.

The other three may agree and offer additional advice from something spotted, which is all designed to help the struggling golfer. The only hope is that the 'know all' doesn't get back into the conflab and offer additional changes after studying your swing closely observed from 'afar' and an ability to provide swing analysis, gleaned from years of experience as a winner. You cannot help but glance at the honours boards and notice that the 'know all' has done 'naff all' and in turn question his knowledge and per-ceived technical expertise.

Harsh, I know but jeez after a bellyful of over-stated opinion week after week it really grinds any-one's gears!

Definitions for Non-Golfers

The conversation about a match, be that fourball better ball, a greensomes battle, a foursomes encounter or a plain old alliance competition and the 'tit for tat' that goes with two pairs playing against the course, there are plenty of one liner's that state the obvious banter.

A big part of the 'group analysis' of the match and whether the banter is accurate or not falls into the 'golf speak' lingo, a language that a non-golfer would find difficult to understand. So for a change the responses under the clichés are what a non-golfer might say or think. For a bit of fun again, but based on reality when you bring a non-golfer wife or partner to an after match dinner.

With no idea and in most cases no interest in the stories it is very probable that they could or would contribute, shocked and disgusted at their interpretation of these classics.

"If I hadn't messed up on the 12ᵗʰ"

Oh that sounds disgusting, messing yourself out on the course!

A plausible reply from a non-golfer, but thankfully the reference is to a mistake not a loss of control of bodily functions.

The specific error identified however is seen as the 'only' reason for the downfall, but if it hadn't happened the 13ᵗʰ the fact is that nobody knows what the outcome would be because, guess what, yes, IT DID HAPPEN.

We will never know, that is the only thing that we do know and moreover we all know that any changes would have skewed the time line as clearly explained in 'Back to the Future' by Doc Brown. An alternate time line would be created and one that we have no knowledge of. Yes it might have made a difference, who knows? None of us.

For example halving the 12th could just have easily resulted in four lost holes, not the fight back that has been factored into the debate. But nah, golfers will ignore the alternate time line and think that the mix of fact and the inserted fiction clearly demonstrates that the loss would have been a win. Ahh well keep on dreaming!

"I must have lipped out five times"
What on earth do you get up to out there...filth!
No, not some form of, well 'whatever' with a name given to it, like ...no I can't commit to any sordid name for a lewd act that I have heard to text, that would be wrong.

'Lipping Out' is not a spelling mistake either, it means catching the edge of the hole with a putt and the ball staying out after following the rim of the hole. Glad we have that sorted.

The thing is that golfers mistake a near miss of under an inch from the edge of the hole and call it 'lipping out' probably because they like the cliché, but that's not important right now.

"Your putt on the 14th was a killer"
Jesus, Son of God, who died?
Once more the alternate definition offered here or interpretation of the comment does suggest that an atrocity occurred on the 14th, death by a putt, not the candlestick in the library by Miss Green.

Thankfully no, the missing word that would have

made this all make sense to a non-golfer is 'blow' a 'killer blow' but on reflection maybe this needs replacing too, say with, 'was rather good, a well won hole, old chap'. Oh sod it keep to the killer blow.

"You finished me off well today"

What the hell! I thought you were golfing not that, you wait until I get you home...

No, no, no. It means that the match was concluded without risk of letting the opponent catch up and get back into the contest. Phew, a close call.

"You really put me in some awkward positions today"

It beggars belief what you really get up to out there!

Oh god, more misunderstood 'golf speak', it means that the dreaded foursomes game played relies on staying in play not being put into the dark woods. Nothing to do with the Karma Sutra!

"I'm glad you knocked me off the card a few times"

Standing on a card and getting knocked off, I didn't realise it was a contact sport?

Yes it sounds crazy, but what this means is after a mediocre score the playing partner betters the effort, not physical contact and the loser being knocked off a pedestal, whether a piece of card or not!

"You were on fire today"

What, how the hell did you catch on fire?

No, metaphorically speaking, being on fire isn't being torched on the course; it refers to playing very well actually. Although where it comes from in such a placid sport is probably never going to be known. Someone will have said it first, who though we will never know!

Having to explain this to a non-golfer takes a bit of further explanation because if you think about how on earth does being on fire mean something good, it sounds incredibly painful instead. A simple reference to being hot probably works as the eyebrows go up in recognition of another stupid description in golf speak.

The Last Word, Or Is It Excuse?

Apart from boring the poor non-golfers that accompany golfers to social functions and get pulled into conversations that make no sense, the fact remains that golfers will continue to develop more off the wall clichés and develop the 'golf speak' language. Indeed the final batch of comments and clichés, if anything, highlight the final overview that takes place in the 19th hole as the fourball finish off their drinks and shake hands, until next time.

"All I needed was a five"

Yes but you made 7, and indeed were playing three off the tee so unless you holed your third it was never going to happen.

The 'all I needed' comment is one that can be heard at every club, every day most likely. The realisation that if the last hole had been kind then with a bogey on the last all would have been so different. Is this the crux of the whole book? I think it is and really reinforces the 'almost' wishes that keep us coming back for more punishment.

"It was uphill all the way"
Looks pretty flat to me, what does that mean?
Aha, the uphill struggle which golfers refer to all the time, and which for most of us IS all of the time. Once again it doesn't make sense to say it save the known fact that anything that is a struggle is often referred to as uphill.

"I left myself with too much to do"
Actually you needed to do less and take less shots in truth!
Doing more equals a better result? Oh no, not in golf, doing less means better scores, so I have never quite grasped the need to do more to do better.... Unless more is less that is... Bizarre.

"It didn't feel right today"
God does it ever feel right, can't say I relate to that one!
It could be that confidence thingy or at the very least the feeling that evades us all. We stand over a shot and something doesn't feel right but we step away far too rarely and start again.

But yes, there are days when the swing feels alien. The set up feels like you have lost an inch or two off one leg overnight or every shot hurts the hands with the vibration from the iron after a poorly hit shot. No wonder it doesn't feel right!

"Maybe next time"
Hope so...for all of us!
No matter how well or how badly a round of golf has gone, the desire to do better next time is the thing that brings golfers back next week to take on the

course and other golfers. Other poor sods that have also been lured back despite the high scores recorded on the card on the previous round.

It is a game that frustrates players to the extreme. A fine line between success and I would say failure but that would be wrong. In a medal round a golfer plays against the rest of the field but also against the course and even if a winning score is unlikely there is always the chance to play close to the handicap trim a little off the exact handicap or stay in the buffer zone.

In a match play contest it is never over until the winning putt goes in and thus there is always a chance to get back in a match.

We all have the ability and potential to hit a freakishly good shot inside us. One's that come from nowhere and that can change a bad day into a very exceptional one and this is why we play the game love it, while at times hating it!

Thankfully the camaraderie and banter has helped develop a language, 'golf speak', to get us through and share our innermost feelings through expressive comments that only make sense to avid golfers. I have tried to reflect 'golf speak' in a book of clichés that keep us amused and thus soften the blow somewhat. After all, without the drivel and crazy comments what a boring game it would be. It is the essence of the game and is the fifteenth club in the bag for many of us!

My only hope is that as we reach the end of this book that some if what has been written has raised a smile. If it has then pass the title on to fellow golfers so that more buy a copy and I can hopefully generate enough to afford the annual membership fees!

Finally, and as I always do for some bizarre reason, I will finish the book off with a bit of Latin. Not sure why I do, maybe it is a bit of superstition in that not putting a bit of Latin in at the end will result in poor book sales.

This superstition started with the first book and is no doubt similar to superstition that started on the golf course as a child. Not that it has made that much of a difference over the years!

A routine to calm the nerves over a crucial shot such as always marking the ball with the head side of the coin, never the tails side or perhaps to put my golf glove in my right back pocket, never the left, in the Farah trousers that were handed down from my brother or a close relative. Not important now, but superstition it is and so if you will humour me with the final quote, some Latin to insight further debate.

This time I have pinched my own Club motto, which has generated much debate over the last hundred or so years for the classicist golfers and their varied opinions on the translation. Whatever you translate it as it is a fine piece of advice, to save penalty shots at the very least.

Servare Modum
Keep Within Bounds

Suggested further reading

"Life of Pie – Nag Pie
(Fifty More Shades of Nagging)
by Chris Gibson

The follow up satirical offering to the hit eBook and paperback 'Fifty Shades of Nagging' that this time discussed the development of a woman in the art of nagging in a journey through life, a "Life of Pie Nag Pie".

Published by alliebooks.co.uk available as an eBook by Original eBooks and Original Writing (UK) Limited available from Amazon, iTunes and all good sites
Bulk order paperback copies are available from the publisher and via Createspace, global distributor.
Parent ISBN 978-1-909429-06-2
ePub version 978-1-909429-07-9
Mobi version 978-1-909429-08-6

"Fifty Shades of Nagging – Most of them Grey!
by Chris Gibson

The first short book penned by Chris Gibson that looked at what couples say to each other in a vague attempt to communicate. Very much a tongue in cheek satirical view written to raise a smile, not over analyse the subject of perceived 'nagging.' Fifty, or so, pages long it is a quick read with over fifty clichés and comments that some might call 'nagging' while others might simply call it 'motivation.'

Published by alliebooks.co.uk available as an eBook by Original eBooks and Original Writing (UK) Limited available from Amazon, iTunes and all good sites
Bulk order paperback copies are available from the publisher and via Createspace, global distributor.
Parent ISBN 978-1-909429-00-0
ePub version 978-1-909429-02-4
Mobi version 978-1-909429-01-7

(Business books by the author)

"Franchising Exposed – A Definitive Guide
for anyone looking to buy a franchise or develop
a franchise concept"
by Chris Gibson

Chris Gibson's first book first published in 2011 and
written to help people looking to start a new business
or convert an existing business into a licensed
franchise partnership. Advice and anecdotes that can
help make the right informed decision

*Published by alliebooks.co.uk available as an eBook by Original eBooks and Original
Writing (UK) Limited available from Amazon, iTunes and all good sites*
*Bulk order paperback copies are available from the publisher and via Createspace,
global distributor.*
Parent ISBN 978-0-9567618-0-4 (paperback 2011)
ePub version 978-0-9567618-8-0
Mobi version 978-0-9567618-9-7

"Selling, it's not a Mind Trick"
by Chris Gibson & Alan Guinn
First published in 2012 and written with co-author
Alan Guinn, a veteran of training people all over the
world via selling seminars. Collectively this book is
a combination of over 70 years experience in sales
and selling with tip and advice that are designed to
help sales executives and the CEO alike.

SELLING
IT'S NOT A
MIND TRICK

*Published by alliebooks.co.uk available as an eBook by Original eBooks and Original
Writing (UK) Limited available from Amazon, iTunes and all good sites*
*Bulk order paperback copies are available from the publisher and via Createspace,
global distributor.*
Parent ISBN 978-0-9567618-5-9
ePub version 978-0-9567618-6-6
Mobi version 978-0-9567618-7-3

"Selling Skills Exposed – Brilliant Sales Techniques"
by Chris Gibson
& Alan Guinn

A revised look at 'Selling, it's not a Mind Trick' published in 2013, with a new 'search friendly' title and to coincide with global availability on Amazon.

Published by alliebooks.co.uk available as an eBook by Original eBooks and Original Writing (UK) Limited available from Amazon, iTunes and all good sites
Bulk order paperback copies are available from the publisher and via Createspace, global distributor.
Parent ISBN 978-1-909429-03-1
ePub version 978-1-909429-04-8
Mobi version 978-1-909429-05-5

"So…You Want to Buy a Franchise"
by Alan Guinn & Chris Gibson

Written for the US market, although it translates to any language this is essential reading for anyone looking to enter the wonderful world of franchising and start a business. Advice on business planning, operation and sales techniques are also included.

Published by alliebooks.co.uk available as an eBook by Original eBooks and Original Writing (UK) Limited available from Amazon, iTunes and all good sites
Bulk order paperback copies are available from the publisher and via Createspace, global distributor.
Parent ISBN 978-0-9567618-4-8
ePub version 978-0-9567618-3-5
Mobi version 978-0-9567618-2-8

"Psyched for Life – A New Guide to Decision Making"
by Alan Guinn

First published in 2001, a short book written by Alan Guinn to focus the reader on how to make effective decisions and avoid procrastination.
Published by Alan Guinn available from Amazon
ISBN 978-0-9712707-0-1

Chris

That is all - 'Happy Swinging' and thanks for reading